W9-AXA-904

11,662

SLEEP
Is for Everyone

SLEEP
Is for Everyone
By Paul Showers
Illustrated by Wendy Watson

THOMAS Y. CROWELL COMPANY   NEW YORK

LET'S-READ-AND-FIND-OUT SCIENCE BOOKS

Editors: DR. ROMA GANS, Professor Emeritus of Childhood Education, Teachers College, Columbia University
DR. FRANKLYN M. BRANLEY, Astronomer Emeritus and former Chairman of The American Museum-Hayden Planetarium

LIVING THINGS: PLANTS

Down Come the Leaves
How a Seed Grows
Mushrooms and Molds
Plants in Winter
Seeds by Wind and Water
The Sunlit Sea
A Tree Is a Plant
Where Does Your Garden Grow?

LIVING THINGS: ANIMALS, BIRDS, FISH, INSECTS, ETC.

Animals in Winter
Bats in the Dark
Bees and Beelines
Big Tracks, Little Tracks
Birds at Night
Birds Eat and Eat and Eat
Bird Talk
The Blue Whale
Camels: Ships of the Desert
Cockroaches: Here, There, and Everywhere

Ducks Don't Get Wet
The Emperor Penguins
Fireflies in the Night
Giraffes at Home
Green Grass and White Milk
Green Turtle Mysteries
Hummingbirds in the Garden
Hungry Sharks
It's Nesting Time
Ladybug, Ladybug, Fly Away Home
The Long-Lost Coelacanth and Other Living Fossils
My Daddy Longlegs
My Visit to the Dinosaurs
The Opossum
Sandpipers
Shrimps
Spider Silk
Starfish
Twist, Wiggle, and Squirm: A Book about Earthworms
Watch Honeybees with Me
What I Like About Toads
Why Frogs Are Wet

THE HUMAN BODY

A Baby Starts to Grow
Before You Were a Baby
A Drop of Blood
Find Out by Touching
Follow Your Nose
Hear Your Heart
How Many Teeth?
How You Talk
In the Night
Look at Your Eyes*
My Five Senses
My Hands
The Skeleton Inside You
Sleep Is for Everyone
Straight Hair, Curly Hair*
Use Your Brain
What Happens to a Hamburger
Your Skin and Mine*

And other books on AIR, WATER, AND WEATHER; THE EARTH AND ITS COMPOSITION; ASTRONOMY AND SPACE; and MATTER AND ENERGY

*Available in Spanish

Library of Congress Cataloging in Publication Data Showers, Paul. Sleep is for everyone. SUMMARY: Elementary discussion of the importance of sleep and what happens to our brains and bodies during slumber. 1. Sleep—Juv. lit.   [1. Sleep]   I. Watson, Wendy, illus.   II. Title.   QP425.S58   612'.821   72-83785   ISBN 0-690-00424-9   ISBN 0-690-00425-7 (lib. bdg.)

1   2   3   4   5   6   7   8   9   10

SLEEP
Is for Everyone

LET'S READ AND FIND OUT

When a horse goes to sleep, its eyelids go down.

When a chicken goes to sleep, its eyelids go up.

When a snake sleeps, its eyes stay open.

Snakes have no eyelids.

When you go to sleep — which way do your eyelids go?

1

An elephant can sleep standing up.

A pigeon sits down when it sleeps.

Pigs lie down to sleep. So do dogs. So do you.
Sometimes dogs curl up. So do cats. Cows don't.

Do you?

A goose can snooze while it's standing up,
   A snake when it's coiled in a heap.
A bat will doze while it's upside down,
   For all of them have to sleep.

My brother Jonathan sleeps on his face,
  Grandfather nods in his chair.
Sooner or later everyone rests,
  No matter how or where.

Some people sleep more than others do.

Babies do a lot of sleeping.

Jonathan is only 6 weeks old. He sleeps most of the time.

He only wakes up when he wants to eat — or have his
  diaper changed.

Caroline lives next door. She is 2 years old.
Caroline goes to bed right after her dinner.
She sleeps all night, 12 hours or more.
She takes a nap in the afternoon, too.

Sometimes Caroline doesn't get her nap.
Then she is cranky.
Sometimes she cries. And throws things.
But next morning Caroline feels fine again—after
  she has had a good night's sleep.

When people are little, they are growing and they
   need a lot of sleep.
When they grow bigger and older, they need less sleep.
Schoolchildren need to sleep about 10 to 12 hours a night.
Most grownups need only 7 or 8 hours.
But babies, children, and grownups—all of them
   need to have their sleep.

Every part of your body has to rest after it does its work.
Your arms need a rest after they carry heavy bundles.
When you run fast, your legs work hard.

They get tired and you have to rest them.
On a hike people often sit down to rest their tired
  feet.

Your brain works hard, too. It never stops working.
When you are awake, it helps you pay attention to
the world around you—
to the sights you see
and the sounds you hear
the things you taste
and smell
and feel.
You can sit perfectly still and rest your arms and
legs and feet. But your brain isn't resting.
It goes right on thinking as long as you are awake.
Thinking is some of the hardest work your brain
does.

15

At night your brain needs a rest from thinking.

It needs to turn off the world—the same way you turn off the light when you go to bed.

Sleep is the time when part of your brain takes a rest.

But other parts of your brain keep working.
When you are asleep, your brain keeps
   your heart beating and your lungs breathing.
Sometimes your brain makes you turn over
   or move your arms and legs.

But your eyes are shut, and they don't see.
Your ears are open, but you don't hear many sounds.
Your brain doesn't think wide-awake thoughts when
   you sleep.
But it dreams. Dreams are mixed-up thoughts.
Some dreams are very nice. Some are funny.
Most of the time you forget them when you wake up.

People get very sick, and even die, if they do not
   have enough food or enough water.
Scientists have tried to find out what would happen
   if people didn't get enough sleep.
The scientists didn't go to bed.
They stayed up all night and all the next day
   and all that night and the day after that.

They became very sleepy. They wanted to go to bed.
It was harder and harder to stay awake.
They tried to read—but they couldn't follow the words.

They tried to look at TV—but their eyes kept closing.
They played games—but they made mistakes.
They forgot things.
It was harder and harder for their tired brains to
   think.

The scientists grew cross and mean.
They got mad at their friends.
They kept walking so they wouldn't fall asleep.
They drank coffee. They kept yawning.

Finally they were too tired to stand up any longer.
When they sat down, they fell asleep.
They couldn't stay awake any longer.

If people stay awake too long, they don't feel well.
Scientists do not know exactly why sleep is good
    for people, but they know that most people need
    it to stay healthy.

Sometimes it is hard to go to bed.

Maybe I want to watch something special on TV.

Or I might have homework to do.

But my mother makes me go to bed.

Sometimes she is cross with me. That's because she
  is tired.

Sometimes I'm cross. That's because I'm tired.

27

But most of the time I go to bed when my mother
   tells me.
It is warm under the covers.
I feel as if I am floating.
Sometimes I curl up.
Sometimes I stretch out and twist around.
I yawn.
I shut my eyes.

My thoughts begin to wander.
I am floating on a rubber mattress in a pool . . .
  or in a balloon high up in the clouds . . .
I think of lots of different things —
  riding my bicycle . . .
  roller-skating . . .
  an airplane high in the sky . . .
  a basket of apples . . .
  umbrellas in the rain . . .
  my dog Whiskers chewing a bone . . .
  waves at the seashore . . .
  garbage cans . . .
  a goldfish . . .
  racing cars . . .

Soon I stop thinking.
I am asleep.

ABOUT THE AUTHOR

Paul Showers is a New York newspaperman and writer of nearly two dozen books for children. He first became interested in making books for young readers after watching his own children struggle with the "See, Sally, see" books of the 1950's ("television's greatest boon," he calls them). His own books, most of them in the Let's-Read-and-Find-Out series, have thoroughly proved that children's books can be both lively and worthwhile.

Mr. Showers began newspaper work on the Detroit *Free Press*. Then came the New York *Herald Tribune*, a brief stint on the New York *Sunday Mirror*, and, for the past twenty-seven years, the Sunday *New York Times*. Mr. Showers was born in Sunnyside, Washington, and has an A.B. degree from the University of Michigan.

ABOUT THE ILLUSTRATOR

Wendy Watson has written, edited, and adapted books for children, and is the illustrator of nearly three dozen books, many of which have been chosen by the American Institute of Graphic Arts for its children's books shows. Born and raised in Putney, Vermont, she now lives in Toledo, Ohio, with her husband and small daughter.